Moments with Oı

LIVING VERSUS GETTING ON

SWAMI DAYANANDA SARASWATI
Arsha Vidya

Arsha Vidya
Research and Publication Trust
Chennai

Published by :
Arsha Vidya Research and Publication Trust
4 ' Sri nidhi ' Apts 3rd Floor
Sir Desika Road Mylapore
Chennai 600 004 INDIA
Tel : 044 2499 7023, 2499 7131
Email : avrandpt@gmail.com
Website : www.avrpt.com

ISBN : 978-81-903636-6-2

First	Edition	: April	2007	Copies :	1000
1st	Reprint	: December	2007	Copies :	5000
2nd	Reprint	: June	2011	Copies :	1000
3rd	Reprint	: January	2013	Copies :	1000
4th	Reprint	: October	2015	Copies :	1000
5th	Reprint	: January	2018	Copies :	1000

Design & Layout :
Graaphic Design

Printed at :
Sudarsan Graphics
27, Neelakanta Mehta Street
T. Nagar, Chennai 600 017
Email : info@sudarsan.com

CONTENTS

Key to Transliteration and Pronunciation of Sanskrit Letters

Sanskrit is a highly phonetic language and hence accuracy in articulation of the letters is important. For those unfamiliar with the *Devanāgari* script, the international transliteration is a guide to the proper pronunciation of Sanskrit letters.

अ	*a*	*(but)*	ट	*ṭa*	*(true)**3
आ	*ā*	*(father)*	ठ	*ṭha*	*(anthill)**3
इ	*i*	*(it)*	ड	*ḍa*	*(drum)**3
ई	*ī*	*(beat)*	ढ	*ḍha*	*(godhead)**3
उ	*u*	*(full)*	ण	*ṇ*	*a (under)**3
ऊ	*ū*	*(pool)*	त	*ta*	*(path)**4
ऋ	*ṛ*	*(rhythm)*	थ	*tha*	*(thunder)**4
ॠ	*ṝ*	*(marine)*	द	*da*	*(that)**4
ऌ	*ḷ*	*(revelry)*	ध	*dha*	*(breathe)**4
ए	*e*	*(play)*	न	*na*	*(nut)**4
ऐ	*ai*	*(aisle)*	प	*pa*	*(put)* 5
ओ	*o*	*(go)*	फ	*pha*	*(loophole)**5
औ	*au*	*(laud)*	ब	*ba*	*(bin)* 5
क	*ka*	*(seek)* 1	भ	*bha*	*(abhor)**5
ख	*kha*	*(blockhead)**1	म	*ma*	*(much)* 5
ग	*ga*	*(get)* 1	य	*ya*	*(loyal)*
घ	*gha*	*(log hut)**1	र	*ra*	*(red)*
ङ	*ṅa*	*(sing)* 1	ल	*la*	*(luck)*
च	*ca*	*(chunk)* 2	व	*va*	*(vase)*
छ	*cha*	*(catch him)**2	श	*śa*	*(sure)*
ज	*ja*	*(jump)* 2	ष	*ṣa*	*(shun)*
झ	*jha*	*(hedgehog)**2	स	*sa*	*(so)*
ञ	*ña*	*(bunch)* 2	ह	*ha*	*(hum)*

ं	ṁ	*anusvāra*	(nasalisation of preceding vowel)
ः	ḥ	*visarga*	(aspiration of preceding vowel)
*			No exact English equivalents for these letters

1.	Guttural	–	Pronounced from throat
2.	Palatal	–	Pronounced from palate
3.	Lingual	–	Pronounced from cerebrum
4.	Dental	–	Pronounced from teeth
5.	Labial	–	Pronounced from lips

The 5th letter of each of the above class – called nasals – are also pronounced nasally.

FROM BEING A SURVIVOR TO BECOMING A CONTRIBUTOR

All living beings are programmed to survive

There is an instinctual attempt to survive on the part of anything alive because that is how all living beings are programmed. Survival implies a few things: air, water, food, and shelter. Everything beyond these basic needs is a plus, even clothing, unless it is necessary for protection from the elements. The human being is also subject to this programming. While every animal seems to be self-conscious, a human being is self-judging and inhibited as well, implying that the self-consciousness in the human being is complete.

Mere survival is not enough for the self-judging human being

Is mere survival enough? If you are not self- judgemental, it may be enough. Or, if you are incapable of self-judgement like the animals it is enough. Once you are capable of judgement, however, you are going to judge yourself; I cannot ask you not to do so. Even in saying, "Do not judge," I am myself judging you as being judgemental.

Once you are self-aware and are capable of judgement, you are bound to judge. Being self-aware, you are going to recognise some facts about yourself, and then see that some of them are not very redounding to your image. They are disconcerting, disturbing. This is a problem. Because of this, you cannot say, "I survived, therefore, I am happy." In fact, there are some people, who say, "I survived, therefore, I am unhappy. When will I die? Is it going to be like this throughout my lifetime?" There is always someone committing suicide somewhere. So it is clear that we cannot just live as mere survivors. I consider that one is merely a survivor when one does not go beyond consumption and the simple contribution of a survivor, like progeny. That level of contribution is made by animals too.

The human being needs to become a contributor

The human being needs to contribute something to transcend, to get beyond being just a survivor. Living at a level beyond mere survival means going beyond the 'survivor psyche' of taking care of one's needs. Contributing to the world by having more children and increasing the population is done without much ado even by the animals. Thus, you cannot just be a survivor producing another survivor. Neither can you just be a consumer and consider yourself a contributor. In other words, you cannot be self-centered and be a contributor. So what is this contribution?

You do not become a contributor just by being an earning member of the family, or just by being a parent. As a parent, you cross the line between being a survivor and becoming a contributor only when you have the leisure to enjoy your child, so that he or she can grow to become a contributor. Suppose you educate your children and bring them up with much care and attention so that each one becomes a contributor, you are then a contributor because you contribute a contributor. You need to have a certain maturity or growth so that you can convert another person into a contributor. But this is not the only form of contribution.

There are varieties of contributions. All that counts is whether you have reached the level of being a contributor. To reach that level your entire psychology, that is, your way of thinking, your way of looking at yourself, others, and at the world, has to undergo a change.

Vidyā-dānam is the greatest contribution

It is also important to understand that contribution is not only monetary. As we discussed, converting another person from the level of a survivor into that of a contributor is a contribution. That is why it is said that among the many *dānams*, gifts or contributions, *vidyā-dānam,* the gift of knowledge, is considered to be the greatest. Whether you directly offer *vidyā* to another person by teaching a language, a discipline of science, or a skill, or indirectly provide a situation for such transference of knowledge to take place, it is a contribution. What kind of *vidyā* should this be? Any *vidyā* is good, but if you are able to give self-knowledge to a person, that is the greatest contribution. This is exactly what Vedanta does.

A true contributor responds to the human society and to the environment

One rises above the psyche of a survivor when one contributes something to the world. This contribution need not be to human society alone. If you have to live your life positively and not just get by, if you have to rise above being a mere survivor, you need to act at a deeper level. This is a level which not only includes the significant others in your life, but is one in which every other person becomes significant to you.

For this, you need to enjoy a certain depth within yourself, a certain strength or intensity with which you respond to the world and the entire environment; every plant, every tree, every organism. It is then that you become a true contributor, and stop being a factor in the problems that are already there.

In order to be aware and sensitive to the human ecology, you need to become free of double standards. This may be your differing responses towards people from your country versus those from another country, or your different attitude towards people who belong to your religious tradition or culture as opposed to those who belong to another religious tradition or culture, etc. You then begin to look at people in general from a perspective that is all embracing and, therefore, do not live a life of resistance, a life of abrasion. The 9/11 terrorist attack on the World Trade Center was due to a theology of double standards. Those who committed the crime are also human beings. They had love for their parents, their children, and their own lives too. But then, at the deepest level, the core religious level, they believe that anyone who does not accept their religious tradition is an enemy to God and is, therefore, punishable. This dangerous belief is purely due to indoctrination. That is why I say that if these types of religious beliefs do not interfere, human beings will have only human limitations and not this additional doctrinal limitation. Human limitations of greed, selfishness, anger, hatred, or jealousy do not create problems of this nature. They do not motivate you to bring about colossal destruction. It is doctrinal conditioning, which can play havoc and even cause a holocaust.

Therefore, it is very important that every human being grow into that person who is not just a survivor, but is one who contributes in a constructive manner and does not add anything that hurts people or hurts the environment.

To live is to be a positive contributor

I consider that living begins when one contributes something that will bring about more joy, more happiness, more light, and more freedom. Until then one merely drags one's life through old age and on to the grave. Just getting by is not really living. To live is to be a positive contributor. *Sevā* work provides an avenue, an occasion, an opportunity for people to care for others. In doing so, one cares for oneself. Something happens to a person when he or she is able to do something for someone else. It is not pride. It is something natural, an inner expansion that is an indication of growth because the essential nature of a human being is fullness, wholeness. This wholeness finds expression when you are able to help others you do not even know, except to know that they need help. In Sanskrit, that person is called a *suhṛt*. When one is a *mitram,* a friend, one helps because of the friendship. A *suhṛt,* however, is one who does something because it is to be done, regardless of whether the recipient is known to him or her.

A CONTRIBUTOR IS COMPASSIONATE

A contributor should recognise oneself as a contributor

It is not enough to be a contributor; one has to recognise oneself as being a contributor. It has nothing to do with seeking others' approval or getting others' recognition. One needs to recognise this fact in one's own reckoning. Merely feeling it would not be enough, for no feeling is going to be permanent. By definition, a feeling is that which is whimsical. The ups and downs that are called feelings have a transient life. A reality about you, however, is not a feeling, but a thing to be recognised. Once recognised, it is true. For this, one has to have a certain level of reckoning of oneself as more than a mere survivor. Even when one is laid off and has no job, a contributor is always a contributor because it is more a recognition about oneself than any given action. It implies a certain degree of compassion.

Compassion is always related to something

Compassion is one word that is generally glossed over. I do not think that there is another word as important in marking a person's inner growth. No other word completely conveys what this single word conveys.

Compassion is a dynamic word. In Sanskrit, we call it *dayā*. It involves discovering compassion towards oneself, towards one's own body, and towards the world in general. Compassion is always towards something. It is always related to something. Related alone the word 'compassion' has being. Unrelated, it does not. *Ānanda*, however, is unrelated and yet, has being. *Ātmanyevātmanā tuṣṭaḥ* is being happy in oneself with oneself alone (Bhagavad Gītā, 2-55). Related, *ānanda* becomes love, it becomes compassion, it becomes giving, and it becomes sharing. It is dynamic and it 'becomes.' So, while the word for the self as unrelated is *ānanda*, related, it is compassion. Compassion is human. Religion should evoke human compassion and not disturb it.

It is an expression of who we are

No other quality makes a person live his or her life without it being a burden, if you can call compassion a quality. Is it a special trait? Is it something acquired by following some practice or method? Compassion is not born of a technique. It cannot be a product, a result of something, because it is just an expression of who you are.

An act of compassion can evoke inhibited compassion

An act of compassion can evoke compassion that may be inhibited. An act is always deliberate. It is different from an instinctual or impulsive response, which is more of a reaction. In a deliberate act of compassion, one acts deliberately, as though one has compassion because one has a value for compassion. If you want to gain some result from appearing to be compassionate, you do not have value for compassion, but are pretending to be other than what you are to serve another end. You want to be the beneficiary of being seen as compassionate. No, I am not proposing that. That is deception and hypocrisy. Instead, here, you have a value for becoming compassionate because you have discovered the value of compassion. An act of compassion without there being compassion, but nevertheless arising from a value for compassion, and in order to discover compassion, is not pretension. That is called living.

Only a compassionate person can contribute

To pass from being a survivor to becoming a contributor, one has to have compassion. Only a compassionate person or a person who has a certain inner space can contribute. No impulsive person can contribute. People would say an act of compassion is helping somebody who needs help. I think this is a simple human action with a degree of compassion. A true act of compassion is deliberate such as when you perceive that somebody has done something wrong to you and yet you pray for that person's welfare. If somebody does you a disservice and yet, you reach out, you cross all the borders of anger and hatred and get into a new territory that you are not used to, that is called an act of compassion.

Ahiṁsā becomes compassion

In Vedanta, a number of values and attitudes are listed as necessary for a human being. *Ahiṁsā* is mentioned in the list given in the thirteenth chapter of the Bhagavad Gītā (13-8), '*amānitvam adambhitvam ahiṁsā kṣāntir ārjavam,* absence of conceit, absence of hypocrisy, harmlessness, accommodation, straightforwardness,' but *dayā* is not mentioned there. It is mentioned, however, in another verse, '*adveṣṭā sarvabhūtānāṁ maitraḥ karuṇa eva ca,* the one who has no hatred or ill-will to any being, the one who has the disposition of a friend, who is compassionate' (Bhagavad Gītā, 12-13). When you look into these three words, *maitraḥ, karuṇaḥ,* and *adveṣṭā,* you see their being in *bhūta-dayā,* compassion for all beings. If you stretch *ahiṁsā,* not hurting, it becomes *bhūta-dayā.*

We have always maintained that among the values of *dharma, ahiṁsā* is the most exalted, *ahiṁsā paramo dharmaḥ.* When you stay with *ahiṁsā* and do not gloss over it, it becomes *dayā.* That is the reason why Mahāvīra and Buddha emphasized *ahiṁsā,* and the Veda highlighted *sannyāsa* or renunciation even before their times. In *sannyāsa,* one's whole life is committed to what we call *bhūta-dayā* or *ahiṁsā.* It is a vow, *na hiṁse,* 'Hereafter, I am not going to cause any hurt to any being.' Therefore, a *sannyāsī* becomes a non-competitor. He moves away from where there is competition.

In competitive societies, we hurt each other

Competition has acceptable rules, which both competitors follow; when I get a chance, I hurt you, though not illegally, and you hit me all right, but never below the belt. We allow ourselves to hurt others, we equip and protect ourselves to hurt others, and they have as much right to hurt us because those are the rules of the game. It is called *pāpa-dravya-upajīvanam.* Our *upajīvanam,* daily earning, is through *pāpa-dravya,* money earned through competition, which is often at the cost of someone else, or sometimes not through fair means. Even in a society where there is no competition, there is some act of *pāpa* associated with earning one's livelihood, but where there is competition, the earning is definitely *pāpa-dravya*. This is the reason we need to pray daily. It is like taking a cleansing bath every day. Because you need to earn your living, you have to have a *vidhikriyā*, an enjoined ritual action, like the daily *agnihotra-karma* or some other *vaidika-karma*. If you don't do any of these, at least do *pūjā*, *kīrtan* or *japa*, or, at the very least, do meditation, so that you get rid of this daily gathering of *pāpa*.

In the non-competitive vaidika society, the goal is inner growth

The more I understand the *vaidika* society, the more I admire it. It is a society with no professional competition. We gloat about competition and opportunities in the modern society. Sure, everyone has a lot of opportunities—to strangulate every other person. The other person has an equal opportunity to do the same, so they both want to defeat each other; it is all part of the game. However, in a society where there is no competition, you definitely need to have some maturity. The goal is inner growth. It is not just survival.

A human being has to grow within, as a person, and it is understandable that in order to do that you try to minimize the competition. So the son of a priest becomes a priest, and marries the daughter of a priest. This is how those communities are. Professionally, it is wonderful because there is zero competition. A snake charmer's son is also a snake charmer, and a snake charmer marries only the daughter of another snake charmer. The son of a *vaidya*, a doctor, is also a doctor. There was no professional competition in the *vaidika* society.

A sannyāsī is the one who is completely non-competitive

In a non-competitive society, growth lies only within. Even in such a society, the element of *pāpa-dravya* is present. You grow out of that element only when you become completely non-competitive, and live the simple life of a *sannyāsī*. That is why this concept of *sannyāsa* was there in the *vaidika* society. What is the vow taken by the *sannyāsī*? What is the life of a *sannyāsī*? What is it that he is committed to?

Sannyāsīs are committed to ahiṁsā and dayā

The *sannyāsī* is committed to *tyāga*, renunciation, which involves *ahiṁsā*, not harming. *Sannyāsa* is *ahiṁsā*; it is compassion, it is *bhūta-dayā*. The commitment is to show compassion towards every creature. A *sannyāsī* is supposed to walk from place to place and stay not more than three nights in a place, but, in fact, he does not travel during the rainy season. Insects such as varieties of beetles and especially centipedes come out during the rainy season. All the paths are full of these creatures, and when a person walks, a lot of them will die under his feet. Because of their commitment to *ahiṁsā*, *sannyāsī*s don't want to kill any of these creatures even unconsciously, and so they do not move about, but stay put in one place during the rainy season. In the *sannyāsa-mantras* we address the trees, plants, and animals and vow not to afflict any living being, *prāṇipīḍā*. These are very serious vows. Therefore, that which marks *sannyāsa* is compassion, *dayā*.

Compassion evokes the pleased self

It is not what you do, but the level at which you operate that makes you a contributor

If you have to cultivate any one thing to be no longer just a survivor, it would be compassion. You perform an act of compassion because you have a value for compassion. You don't have compassion towards somebody when you perceive the person as a threat or as a competitor to you, but you cross the barriers and carry out an act of compassion. It is then that you become a contributor. It is not what you do, but the level at which you operate that makes you a contributor. When you function at that level you reckon yourself a contributor.

Yad bhāvam tad bhavati, when you think of yourself as someone who needs to be protected from others, you become a weakling. When you think that you can offer protection to others, you become strong. If you think that the world is a trap, it is a trap. You will perceive a threat everywhere. Every shadow becomes a ghost and every rope turns into a snake because of this fear. Every benign person becomes hostile and you see hostility everywhere. It all depends upon how you look at yourself. The world is a bully to you if you think you are a victim; it will bully you if you are weak, and negotiate with you if you are strong. The poet Bhartṛhari wrote that the wind, *vāyu*, becomes an enemy to the small flame and extinguishes it, but if the flame is strong, *vāyu* becomes a friend. We see that even a passing wind can extinguish a small flame such as that of a matchstick. However, when that flame is strong, like a raging fire, the wind only fans it on and helps it spread! In this world, people parley with the strong and bully the weak. This strength is not physical, but an inner strength. The world is a friend if you are strong, and if you are strong, you become a contributor. If you are weak, you are at best, a survivor against all odds. You can either be a survivor or you can choose to be a contributor.

It takes honesty to be strong and to be compassionate. People think that if you are compassionate you are weak. That is not so. No weak person is compassionate, either to himself or to the world.

Compassion starts with self-love

One cannot be compassionate to the world unless one is compassionate to oneself. You cannot afford to look at yourself unkindly, and if you look at your body also as yourself, be kind to this body as well. Compassion starts with caring for your body, because when you care for your body, you have self-love. Yoga, consisting of *āsana*s initially, is good because you begin to care for your body. While aerobics is self-violence, yoga is love. The self is lovable, so caring for the body becomes a way of demonstrating your love. By doing something caring you discover love for your self, so in this way, an act of caring becomes an act of love.

We all love the pleased self

The Upaniṣad talks about the sage Yājñavalkya's desire to take *sannyāsa*. He was married at that time and had two wives, Kātyāyanī and Maitreyī. He tells them of his decision to leave. The dialogue between Kātyāyanī and Yājñavalkya is not recorded in the *Upaniṣad,* so we may infer that she must have accepted his decision to go. However, Maitreyī does not leave him that easily. Yājñavalkya tells Maitreyī that he has divided their *vitta,* wealth, equally between her and Kātyāyanī. Here, *vitta* also implies a lot of cattle. Yājñavalkya was a very learned person, and a learned man was always given a lot of land, gold, and cattle, so he had a lot of wealth. Yājñavalkya knew everything about the *ātmā,* the self, but wanted to gain *niṣṭhā. Niṣṭhā* is to make your knowledge real. For knowledge of the self to grow in terms of clarity, a certain contemplative life is needed. Therefore, Yājñavalkya wants Maitreyī's permission to leave the life of a *gṛhastha,* householder and take up *sannyāsa.* Maitreyī has one question for him. She asks if all the wealth that he is leaving behind for her will serve to give her the *mokṣa* or liberation that he seeks for himself, which she also wants. Yājñavalkya is honest and says that it will not give her *mokṣa,* and also tells her why. 'Hey Maitreyī, everything becomes loved for the sake of one's self alone, *ātmanastu kāmāya sarvaṁ priyaṁ bhavati*' (*Bṛhadāraṇyaka Upaniṣad,* 4-5-6). Nobody wants wealth for the sake of wealth. One wants wealth for one's own sake. This insight is a great piece of knowledge that everyone has to know and appreciate.

Yājñavalkya says that whatever you love or love to have, to possess or experience is not for the sake of the object, but for the sake of your own self, which is dear to you, *ātmanaḥ kāmāya*. It is in desiring yourself alone that you desire at all. You always desire something other than yourself because it pleases you, but it is the pleased self and not the desired object that you truly love. We all love the pleased self. If something makes you displeased, you are going to drop it. Then what is it that you love? You love the pleased self, the pleased self that you want to be.

Why is it that you love the pleased self alone? Sentiments such as 'God is love, He loves you' are bandied about, and we accept them without understanding or enquiring into them. What do you mean by 'God is love'? The problem is that nobody understands what love is, nor do they know God. If God is love why did he make the poison ivy or the thorns on the rose? 'Because that is the mystery of God!' I say that we should leave such a God alone. Let him be a mystery or let her be a mystery. We have to understand these concepts properly.

We love the pleased self because that is what we are

As Yājñavalkya teaches, you love the pleased self because that is what you are. He offers something new and generally unknown. People are known to desire wealth, desire power, or desire relationships, but Yājñavalkya tells us that this desire is for something else. He says that the object of desire is oneself; the pleased self, which is you. That is what you want to be. Yet you find that you cannot be pleased all the time because you go back to being displeased, and then somebody or something has to please you again. Yājñavalkya proves that you love your self, the pleased self, because that is the real you. Conversely, that you loathe being the displeased self is the corollary.

We need to drop all the wrong notions about the self by listening to the scriptures

Ātmā vāre draṣṭavyaḥ (*Bṛhadāraṇyaka Upaniṣad*, 4-5-6), the self, my dear, is to be 'seen'. The self, *ātmā*, should not be taken for granted; you should not take yourself for granted. When you take yourself for granted, you do not question or enquire into your understanding about yourself, or even consider that it may be wrong. If you do, and decide to know about yourself, you must have a means of knowledge. Knowledge, *jñānam*, depends upon a *pramāṇa*, a means of knowledge.

It is not for want of a pleased self that you do not know yourself. People mistakenly think that the real self or *ātmā* is some hidden 'bliss' that has to be discovered and known. What does it mean to say so? I do not know. No matter how displeased you are in life, you have had the experience of being the pleased self occasionally. There is a pleased self in sleep and there are moments of joy when everybody has been that pleased self. Therefore, ignorance of a pleased self is no plea at all.

Ātmā vāre draṣṭavyaḥ means that the *ātmā* has to be known by you and for that, *ātmā vāre śrotavyaḥ*, one should listen to the teaching about *ātmā*. For this, you require *vedānta-śāstra*. You need to expose yourself to this teaching so that you drop all the wrong notions that you have about the self and remove all your doubts about the nature of the self. Then, after the teaching is received, it is to be contemplated upon, *nididhyāsitavyaḥ*, so that you have clarity. You recognize that the self is the pleased self and articulate it, 'I am *ānanda*.' The self is *ānanda* by nature, in its very *svarūpa,* so there is no reason to look at oneself in a loathsome way. When one looks at oneself in a loathsome way, everything is bitter. There is, therefore, a reason to own up to oneself.

One should be compassionate towards oneself until one discovers Ānanda

Start with having self-love and self-compassion for the physical body. This self that is self-pleased, *ānanda svarūpa,* expresses itself as love when it relates to the world. Unrelated, it is called *ānanda,* and related, it is called love. That *ānanda* is to be discovered. One should be compassionate towards oneself. There is a reason for you to be loving to yourself until the *ānanda* that you are is manifest in the form of love. In love, there is *ānanda.* The love that you feel in a relationship is relative love and in that relative love, there is only a relatively pleased person. Even that, however, is enough to make this love so compelling. This is all you can expect in *saṁsāra*—the relatively pleased person evoked in a loving relationship. Therefore, when you start caring for the physical body, don't get lost in the body itself. There is so much to look at beyond your physical body. That is why yoga is not merely physical in nature, but is defined as something that leads one from self-love to self-knowledge.

Compassion slowly brings out the pleased self

The more you act with compassion towards the world and the more you discover compassion, the better you can understand how you are self-pleased. This is because your nature is *ānanda.* Even a little compassion will make you pleased with yourself. The pleased self, the person who becomes *santuṣṭa*, satisfied, is an *adhikārin*, one who is qualified for studying Vedanta. A *santuṣṭa* is one who has achieved equanimity with reference to what is gained or lost; he is neither given to elation nor given to depression. That is the right attitude to cultivate. Do not bother about what is not there with you. Gather what you can, and leave aside what you are not able to achieve. You have different things to be happy about. Being a *santuṣṭa* begins with having compassion.

Compassion is an important value to be cultivated

The pursuit of dharma is a human end in itself

It looks as though there is a choice in commanding a degree of compassion. I say this because if someone is compassionate we praise the person as being a saint, which means that the person is very special. This is not acceptable in the Vedic culture. In its vision, everyone has to grow into a saint because *dharma* is, in itself, a *puruṣārtha*, a human end. This is not fully understood. Therefore, let us look into this in greater detail.

The four human ends

Dharma, artha, kāma and *mokṣa* are the four *puruṣārtha*s, the *caturvidha-puruṣārthāḥ*. By definition, that which is desired by all people is a *puruṣārtha, sarvaiḥ puruṣhaiḥ arthyate iti puruṣārthaḥ*. It is something that is desired by all people and prayed for, *prārthyate*. *Puruṣa* means a 'person', implying both male and female.

Mokṣa is the most important human end and it is achieved in this birth

Among the four *puruṣārtha*, the most important, *mukhya*, is *mokṣa*. Why is that so? Let us suppose that you say *mokṣa* means not having *punarjanma*, re-birth. A lot of people would then say that they are not interested in that because they want to be reborn. When I say that *mokṣa* is right now, why should I talk of re-birth? If there is a re-birth, we will work on that too. I am very much here and would like to see that I am free enough to have a limited body, a limited mind, limited knowledge, and of course, limited money. If these constitute limitation, there is no *mokṣa* from limitations because these limitations constitute my being.

The body is limited, the mind is limited, knowledge is limited, money is limited, power is limited, and even influence is limited. Even if you become the President of the United States of America you are still subject to certain limitations. Nobody on this earth, no matter what he or she has, is really a happy person. There is always the problem of how one is going to get out of these limitations and enjoy freedom. Death may be a form of freedom, but then people say you will be reborn, so death is not freedom. You are a traveler and you will be back. Therefore, there is no such thing as *mokṣa* after death.

There are religions, which promote heaven as their ultimate goal. They are heaven-bound and they say that all should go to heaven. This promotion of going to heaven, is it a kind of tourism or what? Am I going there as an individual, a *jīva*? That the individual soul survives the death of the body and goes to heaven is a belief one can have. But will this soul have a body or not? If you have a body of your own, you will continue to have the same problems of the body-mind-sense complex limitation. Even if you have a heavenly body, some other heavenly body is different from your body and there is bound to be comparison and a sense of limitation is inevitable. Further, in heaven, there would be a ruler, and you would be the ruled. Therefore, heaven is not a solution.

If there is something called *mokṣa*, either I am free already or I can never be free. If I am free right now and here, it is only a question of knowing how. That is why people say that *mokṣa* is a *parama-puruṣārtha*, the ultimate end.

Dharma is usually presented as a subserving means for the pursuits of artha and kāma

As a *puruṣārtha, artha* means power, security, name and fame, etc., because they give you a sense of security. You can encash your name and fame in society, so when you consider *artha* you should also include this aspect of influence and power. Some of these things can also be viewed as being *kāma* because they give you a sense of ego gratification, which is *kāma*. So *artha* becomes *kāma*. Music, food, relationships, family – all these, providing some satisfaction, are *kāma*. Any ego gratification, name, fame, and so on, also provides this sense of satisfaction.

The *puruṣārtha*s are to be understood as the means to achieve various ends. There ar e a number of means, *sādhana*s, for achieving these various ends. For instance, getting an education and equipping yourself professionally are the means for the pursuit of *artha-kāma*. Among the 'means and ends, *sādhana* and *sādhya*' in the various *artha-kāma* pursuits, one of the means is *dharma*. They say that you should continue your pursuit of *artha* and *kāma,* but be mindful of *dharma*. In doing so, which is the *puruṣārtha*? Is *dharma* the *puruṣārtha*? No, it is not. *Artha* is the *puruṣārtha* and *kāma* is the *puruṣārtha*. You are told to follow *dharma* when you pursue *artha* and *kāma*. Therefore, in this approach, *dharma* becomes a subserving *sādhana* for the pursuits of *artha* and *kāma*. To say that you have to follow *dharma* in order to accomplish *artha* and *kāma* is paying lip service to *dharma*.

As I listen to people of different religious persuasions, I find that nobody thinks of *dharma* as a *puruṣārtha*, as an end to be accomplished. Even many Indian spiritual leaders do not seem to understand this. They always say *dharma* has to be followed in order to achieve *artha* and *kāma* and that is why *dharma* is at the beginning of the list. This is not correct.

DHARMA IS AS MUCH A PURUṢĀRTHA AS ARE ARTHA AND KĀMA

Dharma has as much of a place among the *puruṣārtha*s as *artha* and *kāma*, the ends that human beings want to accomplish. *Dharma* is also an end to be accomplished. That is the reason why we do not look upon saintliness as something that a special person chooses to have or something a person is endowed with. We do not accept that concept.

AHIṀSĀ IS THE PRIMARY DHARMA

That every person has to follow *dharma* means that every person has to follow *ahiṁsā*; it is of the utmost importance, *ahiṁsā paramo dharmaḥ*. When you follow *ahiṁsā*, *dayā* is inevitable because you cannot follow *ahiṁsā* without being compassionate. If you say '*na hiṁse*, I do not hurt,' it means that you have to have compassion. You can use your will to curb the tendency to hurt. Compassion follows. That is why both Mahāvīra and Buddha highlighted *ahiṁsā*. Therefore, *ahiṁsā* is a *dharma* that occupies the first place.

IN PURSUING DHARMA, YOU ADHERE TO ALL THE VALUES

Satyam is another important *dharma*. In fact, if you pursue any one value, everything else will follow. These values are like noodles; they always come as a bunch. So by following *ahiṁsā*, you follow all the values there are, because you cannot follow one without following all the others.

NO OTHER PURUṢĀRTHA IS TO BE PURSUED AT THE COST OF DHARMA

Dharma is something you have to follow, sometimes, even at the cost of *artha* or at the cost of *kāma*. *Dharma*, therefore, becomes an independent end to be achieved. It does not subserve the other ends — it is an independent *puruṣārtha*.

I have heard people saying that if you follow *dharma*, everything else, including *mokṣa*, will take care of itself. It will not take care of itself, but at least you become ready for self-knowledge, which is *mokṣa,* if you follow *dharma*.

COMPASSION HAS TO BE DISCOVERED TO PURSUE DHARMA

In the matrix of values, compassion, which characterizes saintliness, has got to be acquired. That is why it is important to grow from being a mere survivor, into a person of compassion. How does that happen? For this, you need to discover the compassion within by acting it out. Performing an act of compassion will make you compassionate. There is value for being compassionate in an act of compassion, and if you keep doing it consistently, compassion will be with you.

Compassion, the dynamic form of Ānanda, is our very own nature

Compassion, the dynamic form of *ānanda,* is your very nature. Whether you know it completely or not, you can understand this much — that *ānanda* cannot be anything else. There is no object called *ānanda* and there is no place called *ānanda*. There is no person whom you can recognize as *ānanda*. It is not a given time, and it is not an attribute of an object. There is no place, a magic place, where you go to become happy. You can be happy and you can be unhappy anywhere. Still, you do have moments of happiness and, therefore, you can understand that happiness is not anywhere else except centred in you.

We are happy when we are ourselves, when we do not see ourselves as wanting persons

Some say that happiness is inside you. What does that mean? Is happiness in the mind? If the mind makes you happy, does it mean that when you are sad, there is no mind? Even in having its desires fulfilled, the mind is happy only temporarily. However, whenever you are happy, more often than not, you have not fulfilled any desire. Also, more often than not, you need not fulfill a desire to be happy. So what does this happiness depend upon? It depends upon you. It is not even the condition of the mind. When you do not see yourself as a wanting person, if a situation does not evoke a wanting person, you are happy. It is as simple as that. That is your nature. In fact, you are happy when you are yourself, not when you are what you think you are. That is why self-forgetting becomes so important. When what you think about yourself makes you unhappy, then, self-forgetting makes you happy.

Compassion brings us closer to our true nature

Since you do not make a complaint that you are happy, but you cannot stand yourself when you are unhappy, we can say that the happy person, the person you love to be is yourself. This logic, born of experience, is called *anubhava-yukti*. Your own experience, *anubhava*, gives you a certain *yukti*, a certain line of reasoning, which helps you understand that you are *ānanda*. Compassion is a dynamic form of *ānanda*, and that is the reason why, when there is compassion, you are 'close' to yourself. That is why it seems to be the most important thing.

Compassion makes you a person who speaks the truth

We often hear that *satyam*, speaking the truth, is very important. Nevertheless, you can speak the truth and make everybody suffer because the truth you speak may be unpleasant. You are honest, but when you begin talking everybody runs away from you because you are so brutally honest. Speaking the truth also implies that you need to be pleasant. *Satyaṁ brūyāt priyaṁ brūyāt na brūyāt satyam apriyam* (*Manu Smṛti*, 4-138), speak the truth, speak what is pleasant, do not speak a truth that is unpleasant. Therefore, do not deceive in order to please, but at the same time, do not tell the truth if it can displease people. Just keep quiet in those instances. This is why we have been given a choice to speak or not to speak.

It is important to learn when not to speak. Knowing when to speak is different. Knowing when not to speak is more important than knowing when to speak because often, when we speak, what we say does not matter at all. When speaking does not matter, not speaking is very important. People think that *satyam* is just speaking the truth, but sometimes this can make everybody suffer, including you. It is an indication that you cannot be kind to yourself. Therefore, it is really compassion that makes you a person who speaks the truth. It is not that non-compassionate people tell lies, but a compassionate person does not need to tell a lie, and does not need to prove himself or herself as a person.

Compassion is the most important value to be cultivated deliberately

When I look into the system of human values, what stands out for me as a thing to be cultivated deliberately and consciously is compassion. It evokes the bigness in you, the wholeness in you, the love, the giving, and the understanding in you. It also evokes the gentleness in you. Showing certain gentleness makes such a difference in family life also. All this requires inner space.

Compassion brings caring

We need not be thought-free to discover inner space

The space I talk about is always inner space. If one has this space, one can accommodate people and their limitations; objectivity, compassion, and understanding become natural to the person who commands inner space. The discovery of this space is not to be equated with the absence of thought. Some people think that if they can get rid of thoughts they will have peace; no, they will only have thought-free minds. We do not need to be thought-free; we only have to learn how to enjoy space while still relating to the world. After all, it is in relating that you live your life; unrelated, you are merely alive. It is like being asleep; you are alive, but do not relate to the world. In a coma also, you are alive, but do not relate to the world. So, unrelated, one can at best be alive, and alive, one just survives. In being so, you are a mere survivor and not a contributor.

Discovering the inner space helps us relate intelligently

In order to contribute you need to have compassion, and compassion comes when there is space inside. This is achieved by owning up to a certain reality, a certain fact in relating. Relating is living with this space. It is really a crossing over from being a survivor to becoming a contributor. This is not the kind of space that people seek when there is a problem in relating, when there is too much argument or misperception and trust issues. This kind of high maintenance relationship develops because of an unintelligent way of relating. The intelligent way of relating is to discover space within, even while relating.

Relating to the world is relating to other people, not just objects

In relating, there are two factors. One is what you relate to and the other is you. Without these two, there is no relating. In this relationship, if the object is just a chair or a table, relating becomes easy. It is a one-sided relating. Objects such as a chair or a table do not have a mind, *sūkṣma-śarīra*, the subtle body. Therefore, you can sit on the chair, and you can get off it too. There is no problem. This is not what we mean when we say that we relate to the world. What we mean is relating to the world of people; our elders, our children, our siblings, and spouse. These are all inevitable relationships.

Who we relate to is always a variable

You can discover space while relating if you understand certain realities about any given relationship. The reality of a relationship is that, firstly the object or person I relate to is variable. You relate to different people and hold different types of relationships. That is an important thing. For instance, one relates to one's brother as also to one's sister. One relates to one's father, one's mother, one's wife or husband, and then there are one's children. One also relates to each of one's children separately. Even in a teaching situation where there are many students, teaching is always one to one, so each student is addressed. Therefore, when you relate to different people you relate to each one of them individually. Thus, in a relationship, whomever you relate to is always variable. The same person may also be variable, for a person has moods, good moods and bad moods. That is another variable. And a person, being dynamic, has to be variable. So the truth of relating is that what you are relating to is subject to variation and you are the constant, the invariable.

We also change with respect to each relationship

One has to relate to one's father or mother, one's son, brother, sister, spouse, children, employer, employee, co-workers, and so on. Even though the same person has to relate to all these others, there is a relevant change in him as the related person changes.

In relating differently to different people, I am a son or daughter to my father, and I am a son or daughter to my mother as well, but in a different way. This is because my father is different from my mother in terms of how I relate. This means that there is a father's son and there is a mother's son, just as much as there is a father's daughter and a mother's daughter. Then you have your own spouse, your own children. With respect to each one of them also, you change.

We change hats from one role to another

One thing, however, is constant and this is important. When I am related to my father I am his son, but when I am related to my mother, I am her son and at that point, the father is totally replaced. Then, it is only my mother I relate to. Similarly, my mother is totally replaced when I relate to my wife. The parent is totally replaced by the spouse. When you interact with someone related to you in one situation, every other individual in every other situation is completely replaced. From your standpoint, when you relate to all of them you are the constant, only wearing a different hat because you are a father's son or mother's son, or a father's daughter or mother's daughter. These are all different hats because you assume a different status in each relationship. This is an important fact to recognise.

I am constant, but the related status that I assume keeps constantly changing

In each relationship, we assume a referential status. This is an important fact, which goes unrecognised because in each relationship we become what the relationship defines us as being. As Shakespeare says in one of his plays, 'All the world's a stage, and all the men and women merely players.'

It is so true. The world is indeed like a theatre. In all this, I am constant in every role. The role is not pretension. You don't pretend to be a husband. That is not what I am saying. I am saying that this is very real; it is *īśvara-sṛṣṭi*.

The I, *aham,* is constant, but the related status that the 'I' assumes should be relevant to the relationship, or there is a problem. I am a son to my mother and a spouse to my husband or wife. The status totally changes with each role and there should be no hangover. When there is a total substitution on the one side, the object related to, there is also a total substitution in the status of the person, the subject. However, this change is only in the status and not in *aham,* the person.

What do we get out of this? Space. It is like an actor who signs on to play the part of a beggar or a villain secure in the knowledge that he is not either role. There is space in the very assumption, in the very signing of his contract. That is what we are talking about. That space is not physical. Therefore, where is the necessity for substituting people in our relationships and keeping the mind empty? We need a thinking mind, not an empty mind.

I do not have any problems, only my roles do

When there is space you can make a list of all your problems. Don't show it to anybody, just list them. You will find that all the problems fall under different roles. They belong to the various roles you play. So what is my problem? In essence, I am the basic person and I do not have any problem. All problems are restricted to my roles.

Meditation can help us discover that we are playing roles

"But Swamiji, the problems of the roles are my problems." That means that the role and the person are rolled into one! Think of the actor playing his roles on stage. Everything is only 'as though'. The begging person, the actor, does not think that he is a beggar, and this distance between the role and the person is what I call space. What is this distance? Is it a physical distance, when the person is aware of the space between the role and himself? No, it is not. This is a space of self-awareness. That is why I say that in meditation, it is very important that one is oneself. One has to practice this. Shed all roles and just be a simple conscious person who assumes different roles everyday. It is important that I understand that I am playing a role. Otherwise, the problems of the role become my problems. There cannot be a role without problems.

Every role is fraught with problems. When all these problems become me, I do not feel that I have problems; I am the very problem. How is one to have peace of mind? One has to learn to become familiar with having discovered that he or she is a simple conscious person who plays different roles. Vedanta teaches that this simple conscious being is the whole. It is a big thing; indeed, this being is the cause of everything. There is much to learn about it.

At the very minimum, I would say that if you have awareness of this space, you have leisure and compassion, compassion towards yourself and towards others. When there is compassion, when there is space, caring becomes easy.

You can relate to people from that space. Without it, there is only a crowd; there is no compassion and there is no action, there is only reaction. The way of life is one of acting too, relating and acting. That is what living is, and for that, I need space.

Oṁ Tat Sat

For a list of our other publications,
please visit the website at:
www.avrpt.com

...or contact :

ARSHA VIDYA RESEARCH
AND PUBLICATION TRUST
32 / 4 Sir Desika Road
Mylapore Chennai 600 004
Ph : 044 - 2499 7131
Email : avrandpt@gmail.com
Website : www.avrpt.com

ARSHA VIDYA GURUKULAM
Anaikatti P.O.
Coimbatore 641 108
Ph : 0422 - 2657001
Fax : 0422 - 2657002
Email : office@arshavidya.in
Website : www.arshavidya.in

SWAMI DAYANANDA ASHRAM
Purani Jhadi, P.B.No. 30
Rishikesh, Uttaranchal 249 201
Telefax : 0135 - 2430769
Email : ashrambookstore@yahoo.com
Website : www.dayananda.org

ARSHA VIDYA GURUKULAM
P.O. Box 1059. Pennsylvania
PA 18353, USA
Ph : 001 - 570 - 992 - 2339
Email : avp@epix.net
Website : www.arshavidya.org

Our publications are also available at all leading bookstores and downloadable through the 'Teachings of Swami Dayananda' APP for Android and Apple devices.